C000026131

Ce Journal Appartient

à

37369446R00072

Printed in Great Britain
by Amazon